Teach Your Child to Read

300 Short Easy Sentences

English - Korean

Name 

I Can...

- [ ] read the 1st sentence.
- [ ] read the 2nd sentence.
- [ ] make a sentence from a picture.
- [ ] color a picture.
- [ ] Draw a picture.

The frog is going to a party.

개구리가 파티에 가요.

The happy frog is wearing a green hat.

행복한 개구리는 녹색 모자를 쓰고있다.

Name

I Can...

- [ ] read the 1st sentence.
- [ ] read the 2nd sentence.
- [ ] make a sentence from a picture.
- [ ] color a picture.
- [ ] Draw a picture.

Owl likes to read big books.

올빼미는 큰 책을 읽는 것을 좋아합니다.

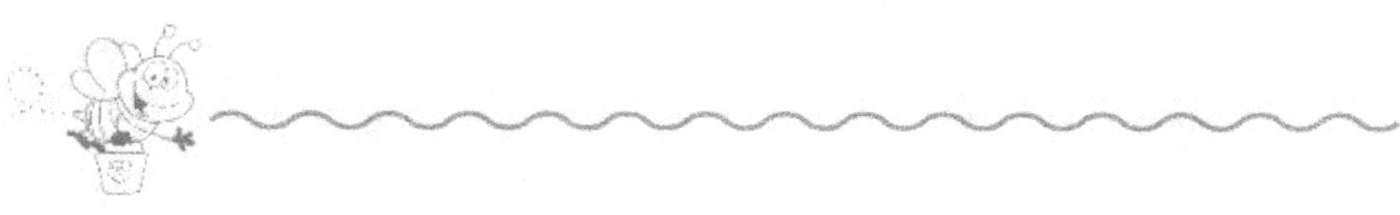

A smart owl is reading an alphabet book.

똑똑한 올빼미가 알파벳 책을 읽고 있습니다.

I Can...

- [ ] read the 1st sentence.
- [ ] read the 2nd sentence.
- [ ] make a sentence from a picture.
- [ ] color a picture.
- [ ] Draw a picture.

Come on! The ice cream truck is here!

어서! 아이스크림 트럭이 여기 있습니다!

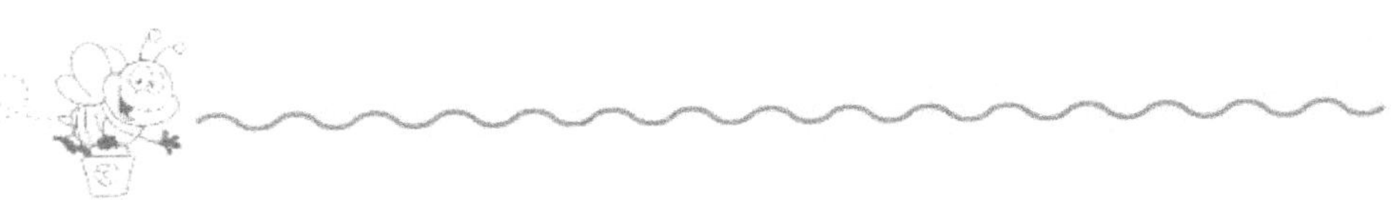

He is driving a big icecream truck.

그는 큰 아이스크림 트럭을 운전하고 있습니다.

Name

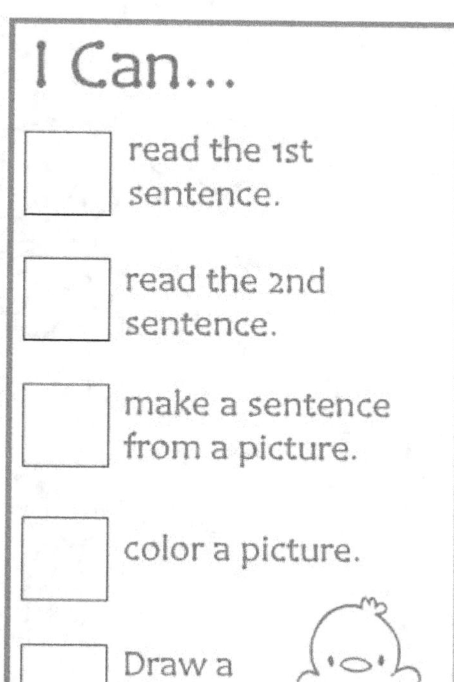

I Can...

- [ ] read the 1st sentence.
- [ ] read the 2nd sentence.
- [ ] make a sentence from a picture.
- [ ] color a picture.
- [ ] Draw a picture.

Dragons are very friendly and have scales on their backs.

용은 매우 친숙하고 등에 비늘이 있습니다.

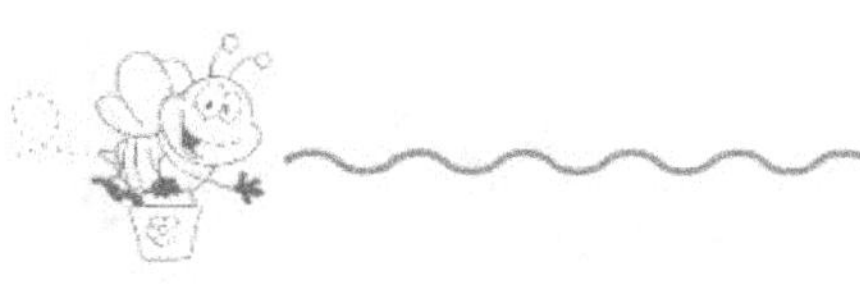

The dragon is waving his hand.

용은 그의 손을 흔들며있다.

Name ____________________

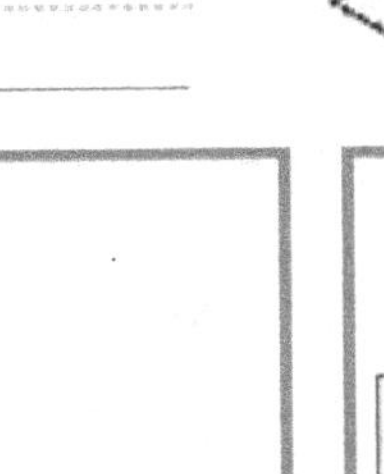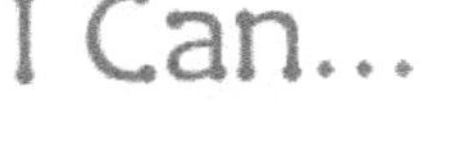

I Can...

- ☐ read the 1st sentence.
- ☐ read the 2nd sentence.
- ☐ make a sentence from a picture.
- ☐ color a picture.
- ☐ Draw a picture.

This ram lives in the farmhouse.

이 램은 농가에 산다.

 ～～～～～～～～～～～～～～～～

Ram has a large horn and fluffy wool.

램은 큰 뿔과 푹신한 양모를 가지고 있습니다.

Name _______________

I Can...

- [ ] read the 1st sentence.
- [ ] read the 2nd sentence.
- [ ] make a sentence from a picture.
- [ ] color a picture.
- [ ] Draw a picture.

The bunny likes to eat carrots.

토끼는 당근을 좋아합니다.

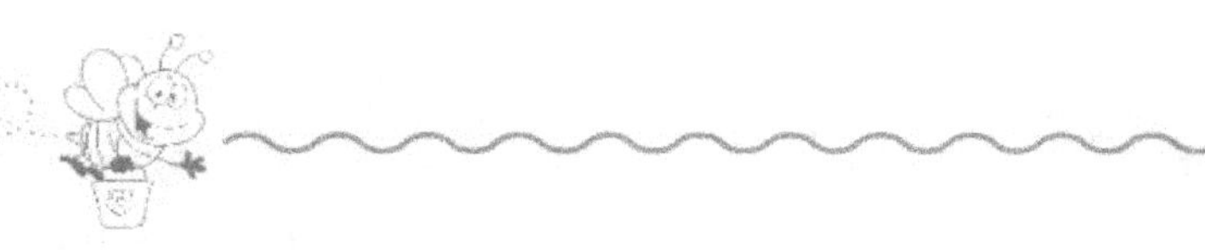

Rabbit thinks that the juicy orange carrot looks yummy.

토끼는 육즙이 많은 주황색 당근이 맛있어 보인다고
생각합니다.

Name ______________________

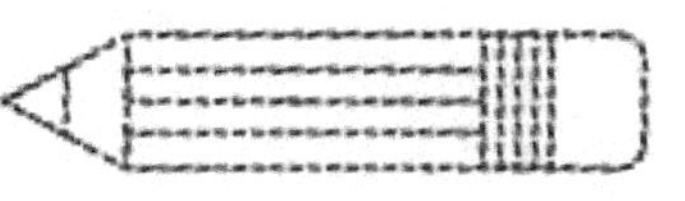

I Can...

- [ ] read the 1st sentence.
- [ ] read the 2nd sentence.
- [ ] make a sentence from a picture.
- [ ] color a picture.
- [ ] Draw a picture.

The clown likes to give out balloons to little kids.

광대는 어린 아이들에게 풍선을주는 것을 좋아합니다.

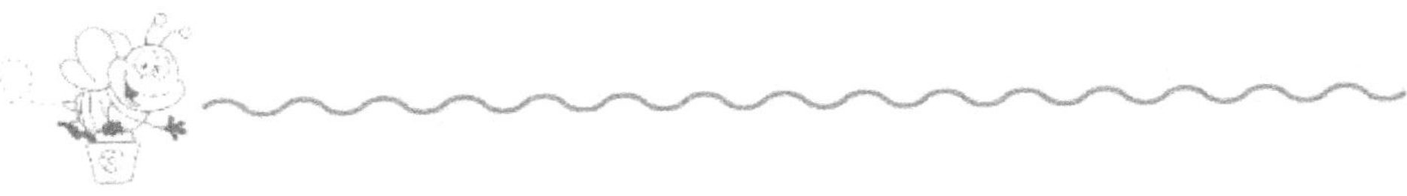

Funny, Mr. Clown is giving away colorful balloons.

재미 있고, 광대 씨는 다채로운 풍선을 선물하고 있습니다.

I Can...

- [ ] read the 1st sentence.
- [ ] read the 2nd sentence.
- [ ] make a sentence from a picture.
- [ ] color a picture.
- [ ] Draw a picture.

The clown is juggling balls for his performance.

광대는 그의 공연으로 공을 저글링하고 있습니다.

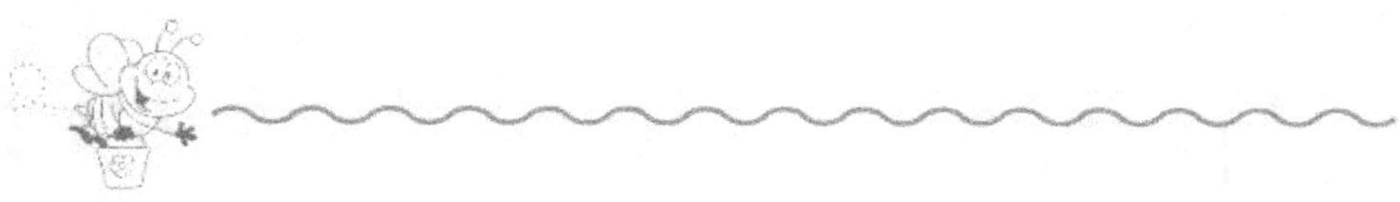

Talented, Mr. Clown is juggling five red balls.

재능있는 광대 씨는 5 개의 빨간 공을 저글링하고 있습니다.

Name

I Can...

- [ ] read the 1st sentence.
- [ ] read the 2nd sentence.
- [ ] make a sentence from a picture.
- [ ] color a picture.
- [ ] Draw a picture.

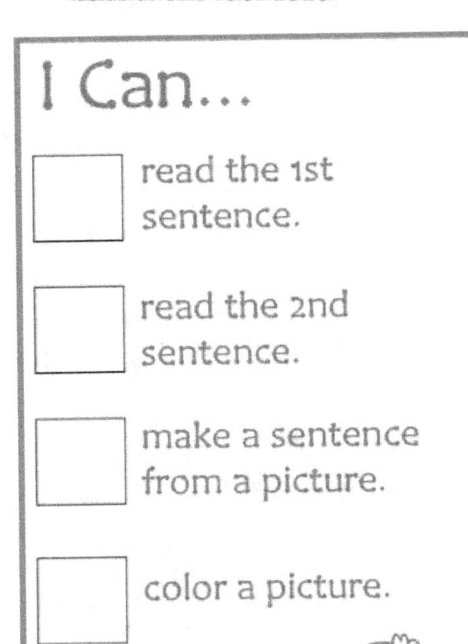

The Easter Bunny is going to give out chocolate eggs.

부활절 토끼는 초콜릿 달걀을 줄 것입니다.

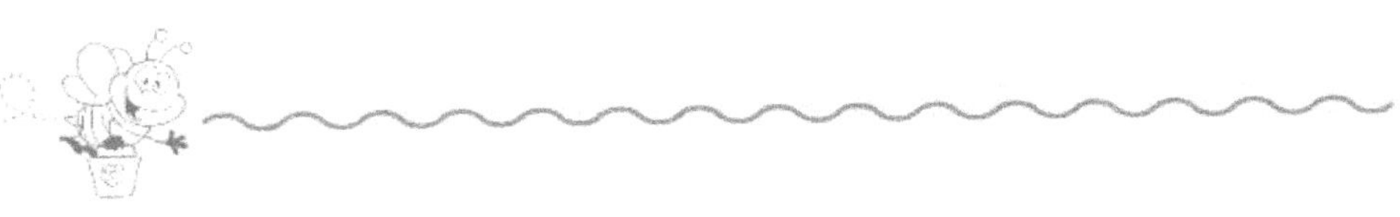

The rabbit goes out to buy more orange carrots.

토끼는 주황색 당근을 더 사러 나갑니다.

Name 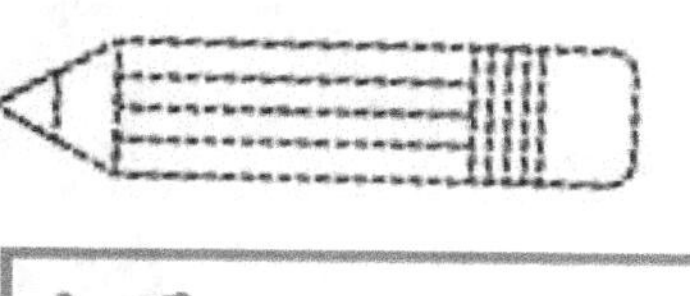

I Can...

- [ ] read the 1st sentence.
- [ ] read the 2nd sentence.
- [ ] make a sentence from a picture.
- [ ] color a picture.
- [ ] Draw a picture.

The pencil is drawing a zig-zag line.

연필이 지그재그 선을 그립니다.

The Pencil is saying hello to you.

연필이 당신에게 인사하고 있습니다.

Name ____________________

I Can...

- [ ] read the 1st sentence.
- [ ] read the 2nd sentence.
- [ ] make a sentence from a picture.
- [ ] color a picture.
- [ ] Draw a picture.

The pencil put on a big smile and went to work.

연필이 크게 웃으며 일하러 갔다.

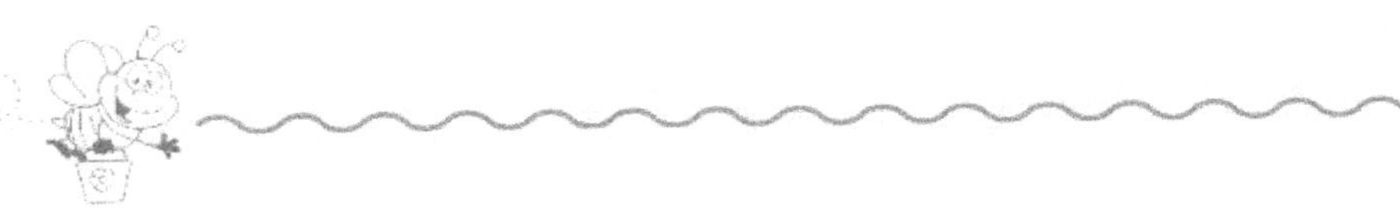

The Pencil is leaving to go on a long relaxing vacation.

연필은 오랫동안 편안한 휴가를 떠나고 있습니다.

Name

I Can...

- ☐ read the 1st sentence.
- ☐ read the 2nd sentence.
- ☐ make a sentence from a picture.
- ☐ color a picture.
- ☐ Draw a picture.

This snowman is my friend, and he is a helper of Santa.

이 눈사람은 내 친구이고 산타의 도우미입니다.

Mr. Snowman is celebrating Christmas by the decorated tree.

눈사람 씨는 장식 된 나무로 크리스마스를 축하합니다.

Name

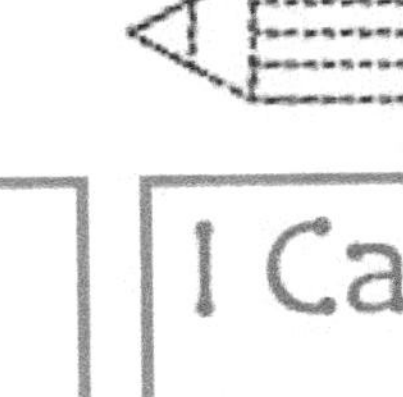

I Can...

- [ ] read the 1st sentence.
- [ ] read the 2nd sentence.
- [ ] make a sentence from a picture.
- [ ] color a picture.
- [ ] Draw a picture.

The octopus is working as a chef and serving food.

문어는 요리사로 일하고 음식을 제공합니다.

Chef Octopus is serving a delicious turkey dinner.

Chef Octopus는 맛있는 칠면조 저녁 식사를 제공합니다.

Name

I Can...

- [ ] read the 1st sentence.
- [ ] read the 2nd sentence.
- [ ] make a sentence from a picture.
- [ ] color a picture.
- [ ] Draw a picture.

Santa is happy.

산타는 행복하다.

Santa Claus is giving extraordinary presents to excited kids.

산타 클로스는 흥분된 아이들에게 특별한
선물을주고 있습니다.

Name 

I Can...

- [ ] read the 1st sentence.
- [ ] read the 2nd sentence.
- [ ] make a sentence from a picture.
- [ ] color a picture.
- [ ] Draw a picture.

The bear likes to eat sweets.

곰은 과자를 좋아합니다.

Teddy is licking a red and white candy cane.

테디는 빨간색과 흰색 사탕 지팡이를 핥고 있습니다.

Name ______________________

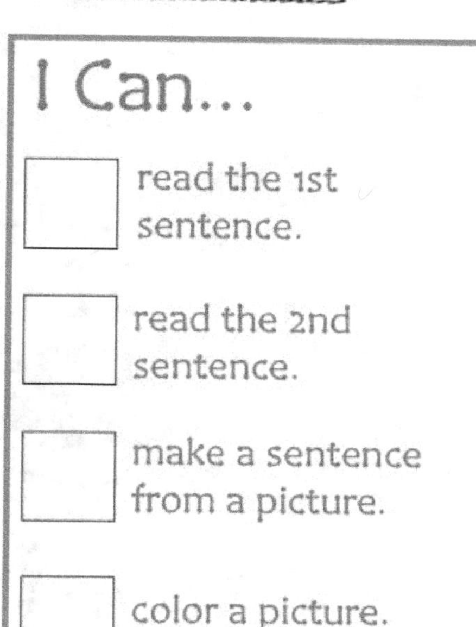

I Can...

- [ ] read the 1st sentence.
- [ ] read the 2nd sentence.
- [ ] make a sentence from a picture.
- [ ] color a picture.
- [ ] Draw a picture.

The book has a wand.

이 책에는 지팡이가 있습니다.

 ~~~~~~~~~~~~~~~~~~~~~~~~~~~~~~~~~~~~~~~

The cereal box got a magician set for Christmas.

시리얼 박스에는 크리스마스 마술사 세트가 있습니다.

Name

I Can...

- [ ] read the 1st sentence.
- [ ] read the 2nd sentence.
- [ ] make a sentence from a picture.
- [ ] color a picture.
- [ ] Draw a picture.

The bear has a present.

곰 선물이 있습니다.

Happy Teddy is opening his box of presents from Santa.

해피 테디는 산타의 선물 상자를 열고있다.

Name 

Santa is going to give out presents.

산타는 선물을 줄 것이다.

Santa is lugging a large brown bag of gifts to his sley.

산타는 그의 갈색 머리에 큰 갈색 가방을
선물하고있다.

Name

I Can...

- ☐ read the 1st sentence.
- ☐ read the 2nd sentence.
- ☐ make a sentence from a picture.
- ☐ color a picture.
- ☐ Draw a picture.

I made a snowman.

나는 눈사람을 만들었습니다.

Mr. Snowman is holding a broom and saying goodbye.

눈사람 씨는 빗자루를 들고 작별 인사를하고 있습니다.

Name

I Can...

- [ ] read the 1st sentence.
- [ ] read the 2nd sentence.
- [ ] make a sentence from a picture.
- [ ] color a picture.
- [ ] Draw a picture.

The parrot is colorful.

앵무새는 화려하다.

The green parrot came from the forest to the zoo.

녹색 앵무새는 숲에서 동물원으로왔다.

Name

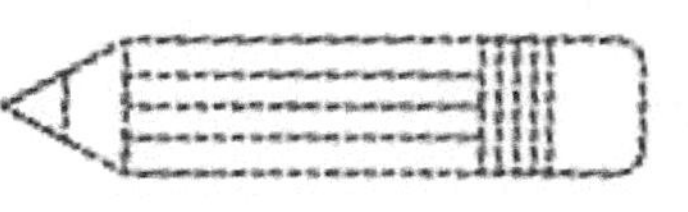

I Can...

- [ ] read the 1st sentence.
- [ ] read the 2nd sentence.
- [ ] make a sentence from a picture.
- [ ] color a picture.
- [ ] Draw a picture.

There are a lot of animals.

많은 동물이 있습니다.

The animals are happy being together again.

동물들은 다시 함께 행복합니다.

Name 

I Can...

- ☐ read the 1st sentence.
- ☐ read the 2nd sentence.
- ☐ make a sentence from a picture.
- ☐ color a picture.
- ☐ Draw a picture.

The man is wearing a belt.

남자는 벨트를 입고있다.

The carpenter is fixing something.

목수가 무언가를 고치고 있습니다.

Name 

I Can...

- [ ] read the 1st sentence.
- [ ] read the 2nd sentence.
- [ ] make a sentence from a picture.
- [ ] color a picture.
- [ ] Draw a picture.

The rabbit is very young.

토끼는 아주 어리다.

The magician plays a trick.

마술사는 마술을합니다.

Name

I Can...

- ☐ read the 1st sentence.
- ☐ read the 2nd sentence.
- ☐ make a sentence from a picture.
- ☐ color a picture.
- ☐ Draw a picture.

He has a potion.

그는 물약이 있습니다.

The scientist is making a potion.

과학자는 물약을 만들고 있습니다.

Name

I Can...

- [ ] read the 1st sentence.
- [ ] read the 2nd sentence.
- [ ] make a sentence from a picture.
- [ ] color a picture.
- [ ] Draw a picture.

He is wearing sunglasses.

그는 선글라스를 쓰고있다.

The policeman is mad.

경찰관이 화났다.

I Can...

- [ ] read the 1st sentence.
- [ ] read the 2nd sentence.
- [ ] make a sentence from a picture.
- [ ] color a picture.
- [ ] Draw a picture.

He has a bucket of paint.

그는 물통이 있습니다.

He likes to paint.

그는 그림을 좋아합니다.

Name

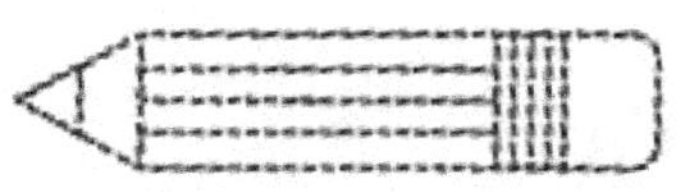

I Can...

- [ ] read the 1st sentence.
- [ ] read the 2nd sentence.
- [ ] make a sentence from a picture.
- [ ] color a picture.
- [ ] Draw a picture.

The man has a hat.

남자는 모자를 가지고있다.

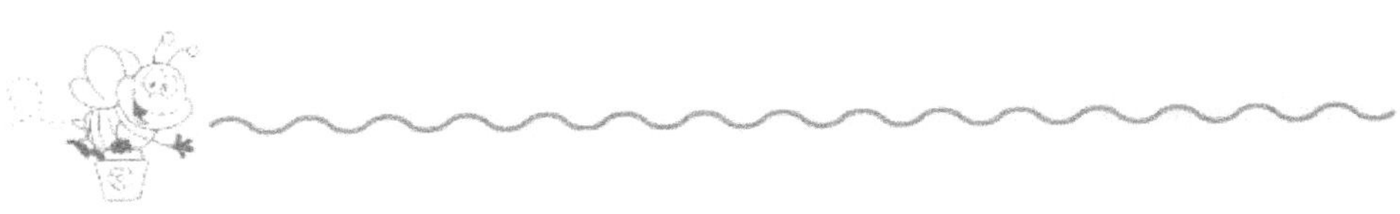

The postman is giving out the mail in the early morning.

우체부는 이른 아침에 우편물을 나눠주고 있습니다.

Name

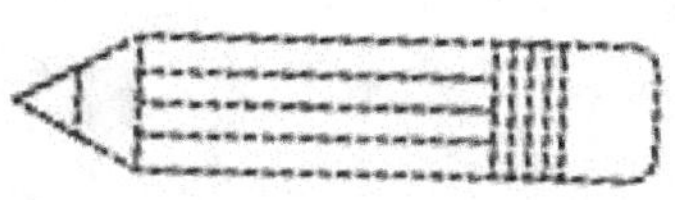

I Can...

- [ ] read the 1st sentence.
- [ ] read the 2nd sentence.
- [ ] make a sentence from a picture.
- [ ] color a picture.
- [ ] Draw a picture.

He has a walkie talkie.

그는 무전기가 있습니다.

He is going to work with his suitcase.

그는 가방을 가지고 일할 것입니다.

Name

I Can...

- [ ] read the 1st sentence.
- [ ] read the 2nd sentence.
- [ ] make a sentence from a picture.
- [ ] color a picture.
- [ ] Draw a picture.

He is sleepy.

그는 졸려요.

The delivery man sent us a package.

배달원이 우리에게 패키지를 보냈습니다.

Name

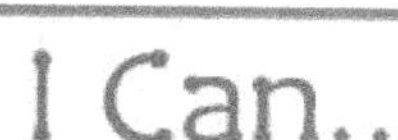

I Can...

- [ ] read the 1st sentence.
- [ ] read the 2nd sentence.
- [ ] make a sentence from a picture.
- [ ] color a picture.
- [ ] Draw a picture.

He is wearing a bowtie.

그는 bowtie를 입고있다.

The waiter is serving juice.

웨이터가 주스를 제공하고 있습니다.

Name

I Can...

- [ ] read the 1st sentence.
- [ ] read the 2nd sentence.
- [ ] make a sentence from a picture.
- [ ] color a picture.
- [ ] Draw a picture.

He has a suitcase.

그는 여행 가방을 가지고있다.

The engineer is holding a wrench.

엔지니어가 렌치를 잡고 있습니다.

Name

I Can...

- [ ] read the 1st sentence.
- [ ] read the 2nd sentence.
- [ ] make a sentence from a picture.
- [ ] color a picture.
- [ ] Draw a picture.

The chef has a napkin.

요리사는 냅킨을 가지고 있습니다.

The chef serves delicious-looking food.

요리사는 맛있는 음식을 제공합니다.

Name

I Can...

- [ ] read the 1st sentence.
- [ ] read the 2nd sentence.
- [ ] make a sentence from a picture.
- [ ] color a picture.
- [ ] Draw a picture.

The rooster has a big beak.

수탉은 큰 부리를 가지고 있습니다.

The chicken is saying hello to us.

닭이 우리에게 인사하고 있습니다.

Name

I Can...

- [ ] read the 1st sentence.
- [ ] read the 2nd sentence.
- [ ] make a sentence from a picture.
- [ ] color a picture.
- [ ] Draw a picture.

The bird is small.

새가 작습니다.

The chick is on the telephone talking with his friend.

병아리가 전화로 친구와 이야기하고 있습니다.

Name

I Can...

- ☐ read the 1st sentence.
- ☐ read the 2nd sentence.
- ☐ make a sentence from a picture.
- ☐ color a picture.
- ☐ Draw a picture.

That is my ring.

그게 내 반지 야

That is a beautiful ring.

아름다운 반지입니다.

Name

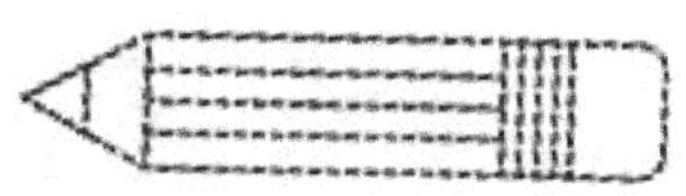

I Can...

- [ ] read the 1st sentence.
- [ ] read the 2nd sentence.
- [ ] make a sentence from a picture.
- [ ] color a picture.
- [ ] Draw a picture.

The duck has three eggs.

오리에는 3 개의 알이 있습니다.

The duck has a big nose.

오리는 큰 코를 가지고 있습니다.

Name

I Can...

- [ ] read the 1st sentence.
- [ ] read the 2nd sentence.
- [ ] make a sentence from a picture.
- [ ] color a picture.
- [ ] Draw a picture.

The swan is beautiful.

백조가 아름답습니다.

The graceful swan is striding through the water.

우아한 백조가 물을 뚫고 있습니다.

Name

I Can...

- [ ] read the 1st sentence.
- [ ] read the 2nd sentence.
- [ ] make a sentence from a picture.
- [ ] color a picture.
- [ ] Draw a picture.

The girl is wearing a dress.

여자 아이가 드레스를 입 었어요.

The maid is cleaning our room.

가정부가 우리 방을 청소하고 있습니다.

Name

I Can...

- [ ] read the 1st sentence.
- [ ] read the 2nd sentence.
- [ ] make a sentence from a picture.
- [ ] color a picture.
- [ ] Draw a picture.

The boy is running.

소년이 달려요.

The little boy was running.

어린 소년이 달리고있었습니다.

Name

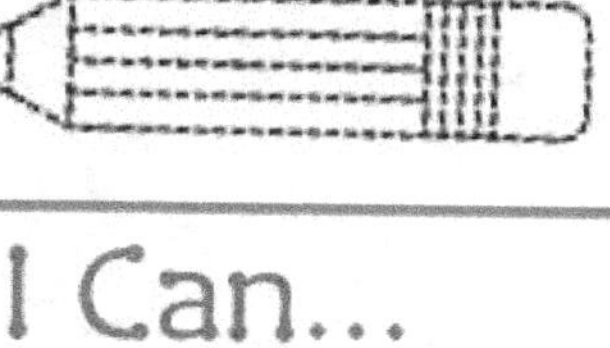

I Can...

- [ ] read the 1st sentence.
- [ ] read the 2nd sentence.
- [ ] make a sentence from a picture.
- [ ] color a picture.
- [ ] Draw a picture.

He is a musician.

그는 음악가입니다.

He is playing a lively tune on his flute.

그는 그의 플루트에서 활발한 곡을 연주하고 있습니다.

Name

I Can...

- [ ] read the 1st sentence.
- [ ] read the 2nd sentence.
- [ ] make a sentence from a picture.
- [ ] color a picture.
- [ ] Draw a picture.

He looks joyful.

그는 즐거워 보인다.

That boy works in a band and plays the drum.

그 소년은 밴드에서 일하고 드럼을 연주합니다.

Name

I Can...

- [ ] read the 1st sentence.
- [ ] read the 2nd sentence.
- [ ] make a sentence from a picture.
- [ ] color a picture.
- [ ] Draw a picture.

The dinosaur is a rock star.

공룡은 록 스타입니다.

The dragon is playing the guitar.

용이 기타를 연주하고 있습니다.

Name

I Can...

- [ ] read the 1st sentence.
- [ ] read the 2nd sentence.
- [ ] make a sentence from a picture.
- [ ] color a picture.
- [ ] Draw a picture.

The nurse helps the doctor.

간호사가 의사를 돕습니다.

The nurse looks scary, holding a syringe.

간호사가 주사기를 들고 무서운 것처럼 보입니다.

Name

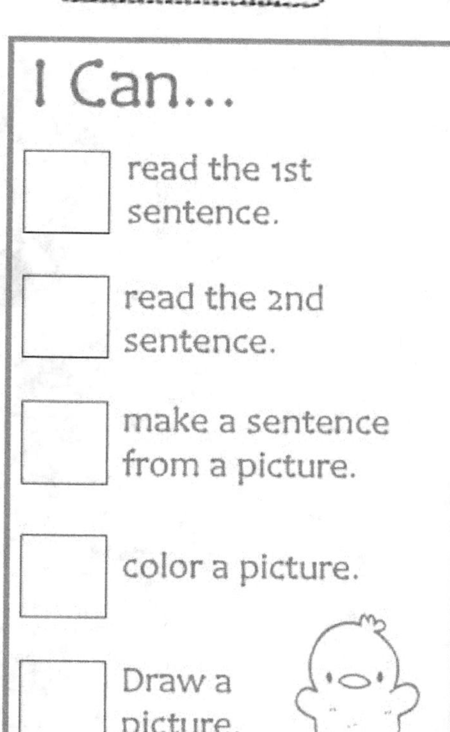

I Can...

- [ ] read the 1st sentence.
- [ ] read the 2nd sentence.
- [ ] make a sentence from a picture.
- [ ] color a picture.
- [ ] Draw a picture.

She is wearing a crown.

그녀는 왕관을 쓰고있다.

The queen bee has a beautiful wand.

여왕벌에는 아름다운 지팡이가 있습니다.

Name

I Can...

- [ ] read the 1st sentence.
- [ ] read the 2nd sentence.
- [ ] make a sentence from a picture.
- [ ] color a picture.
- [ ] Draw a picture.

It is orange and black.

주황색과 검은 색입니다.

The tiger is wearing a bow on its neck.

호랑이가 목에 활을 끼고 있습니다.

Name ___________________________ 

I Can...

- [ ] read the 1st sentence.
- [ ] read the 2nd sentence.
- [ ] make a sentence from a picture.
- [ ] color a picture.
- [ ] Draw a picture.

The boy is carrying a lot of books.

소년은 많은 책을 가지고있다.

 ~~~~~~~~~~~~~~~~~~~~~~~~~~~~~~~~

The boy is carrying so many books!

소년은 너무 많은 책을 가지고있다!

Name

I Can...

- [ ] read the 1st sentence.
- [ ] read the 2nd sentence.
- [ ] make a sentence from a picture.
- [ ] color a picture.
- [ ] Draw a picture.

The pizza looks delicious.

피자가 맛있어 보인다.

The waiter is serving steaming hot pizza.

웨이터가 김이 나는 뜨거운 피자를 제공하고 있습니다.

I Can...

- [ ] read the 1st sentence.
- [ ] read the 2nd sentence.
- [ ] make a sentence from a picture.
- [ ] color a picture.
- [ ] Draw a picture.

That is my dad's computer.

우리 아빠 컴퓨터 야

My dad works on the computer.

아빠는 컴퓨터에서 일 해요.

Name

I Can...

- [ ] read the 1st sentence.
- [ ] read the 2nd sentence.
- [ ] make a sentence from a picture.
- [ ] color a picture.
- [ ] Draw a picture.

The farmer has a beard.

농부는 수염이 있습니다.

The gardener is going to plant flowers

정원사는 꽃을 심을 것입니다

Name

I Can...

- [ ] read the 1st sentence.
- [ ] read the 2nd sentence.
- [ ] make a sentence from a picture.
- [ ] color a picture.
- [ ] Draw a picture.

The strawberry is red.

딸기는 빨간색입니다.

I love to drink strawberry juice.

나는 딸기 주스를 마시는 것을 좋아합니다.

Name

I Can...

- [ ] read the 1st sentence.
- [ ] read the 2nd sentence.
- [ ] make a sentence from a picture.
- [ ] color a picture.
- [ ] Draw a picture.

The magician has a wand.

마술사는 지팡이를 가지고있다.

The wizard likes to work with magic.

마법사는 마술을 좋아합니다.

Name

I Can...

- [ ] read the 1st sentence.
- [ ] read the 2nd sentence.
- [ ] make a sentence from a picture.
- [ ] color a picture.
- [ ] Draw a picture.

Reindeer has a scarf.

순록에는 스카프가 있습니다.

Santa gave reindeer a big present.

산타는 순록에게 큰 선물을 주었다.

Name ___________________

I Can...

- [ ] read the 1st sentence.
- [ ] read the 2nd sentence.
- [ ] make a sentence from a picture.
- [ ] color a picture.
- [ ] Draw a picture.

I have a lot of pencils.

나는 많은 연필이있다.

I have a lot of brushes and pencils.

브러시와 연필이 많이 있습니다.

Name

I Can...

- [ ] read the 1st sentence.
- [ ] read the 2nd sentence.
- [ ] make a sentence from a picture.
- [ ] color a picture.
- [ ] Draw a picture.

Santa is fat.

산타는 뚱뚱하다.

Santa is having fun.

산타가 재밌어요.

Name

I Can...

- [ ] read the 1st sentence.
- [ ] read the 2nd sentence.
- [ ] make a sentence from a picture.
- [ ] color a picture.
- [ ] Draw a picture.

I have one nose.

코가 하나 있습니다.

The one is saying its name.

하나는 그 이름을 말하고 있습니다.

I Can...

- [ ] read the 1st sentence.
- [ ] read the 2nd sentence.
- [ ] make a sentence from a picture.
- [ ] color a picture.
- [ ] Draw a picture.

I have two ears.

두 귀가 있습니다.

The number "two" is holding up bunny ears.

숫자 "2"는 토끼 귀를 잡고 있습니다.

Name

I Can...

- [ ] read the 1st sentence.
- [ ] read the 2nd sentence.
- [ ] make a sentence from a picture.
- [ ] color a picture.
- [ ] Draw a picture.

I have three buttons on my dress.

드레스에 버튼이 3 개 있습니다.

The number "three" is saying you got 3 out of 3.

숫자 "3"은 3에서 3을 얻었음을 나타냅니다.

Name

I Can...

- [ ] read the 1st sentence.
- [ ] read the 2nd sentence.
- [ ] make a sentence from a picture.
- [ ] color a picture.
- [ ] Draw a picture.

I have 0 tails.

꼬리가 0 개 있습니다.

The number "zero" is saying, Ok.

숫자 "0"은 알겠습니다.

Name

I Can...

- [ ] read the 1st sentence.
- [ ] read the 2nd sentence.
- [ ] make a sentence from a picture.
- [ ] color a picture.
- [ ] Draw a picture.

I have five fingers on 1 of my hands.

내 손 중 하나에 다섯 손가락이 있습니다.

The number "five" is trying to give you a high five.

숫자 "five"는 당신에게 하이 파이브를 주려고합니다.

Name

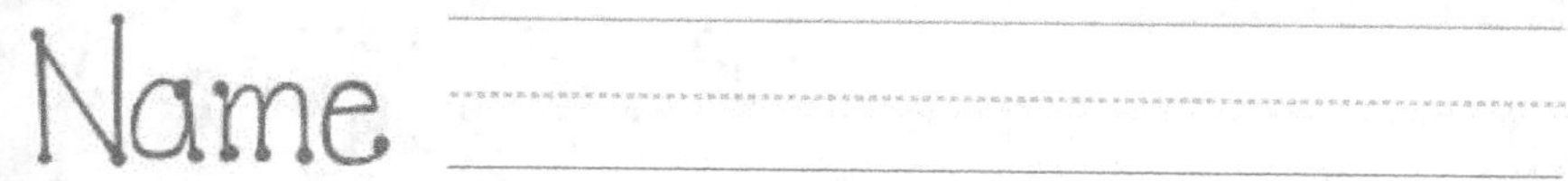

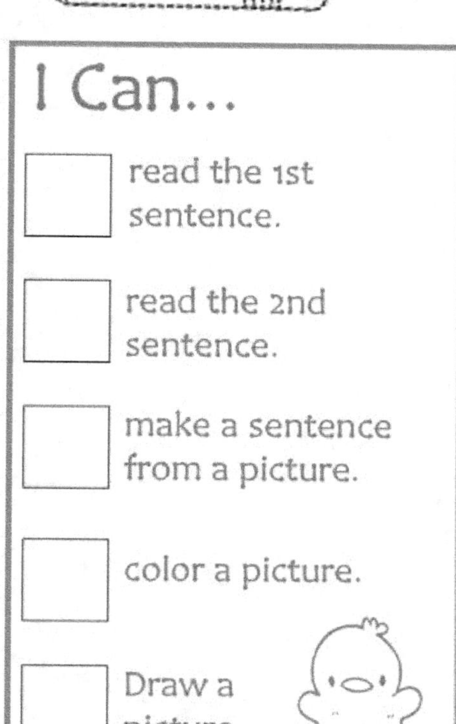

I Can...

- [ ] read the 1st sentence.
- [ ] read the 2nd sentence.
- [ ] make a sentence from a picture.
- [ ] color a picture.
- [ ] Draw a picture.

My cat has four legs.

내 고양이는 네 다리가 있습니다.

The number "four" is counting to four.

숫자 "four"는 4로 계산됩니다.

Name

I Can...

- [ ] read the 1st sentence.
- [ ] read the 2nd sentence.
- [ ] make a sentence from a picture.
- [ ] color a picture.
- [ ] Draw a picture.

A butterfly has six legs.

나비에는 6 개의 다리가 있습니다.

The number "six" is saying 1+5=6.

숫자 "6"은 1 + 5 = 6입니다.

Name

I Can...

- [ ] read the 1st sentence.
- [ ] read the 2nd sentence.
- [ ] make a sentence from a picture.
- [ ] color a picture.
- [ ] Draw a picture.

A spider has eight legs.

거미는 다리가 8 개입니다.

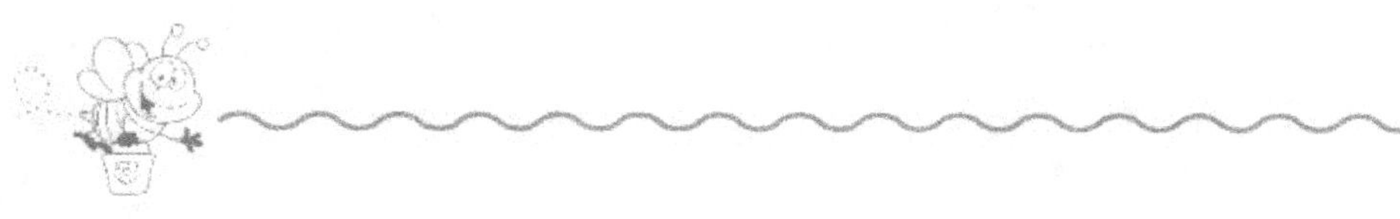

The happy and excited eight is holding up eight fingers

행복하고 흥분된 여덟은 여덟 손가락을 들고있다

Name

I Can...

- [ ] read the 1st sentence.
- [ ] read the 2nd sentence.
- [ ] make a sentence from a picture.
- [ ] color a picture.
- [ ] Draw a picture.

The rooster is going to wake people up.

수탉은 사람들을 깨울 것입니다.

The rooster is on the fence.

수탉은 울타리에 있습니다.

I Can...

- [ ] read the 1st sentence.
- [ ] read the 2nd sentence.
- [ ] make a sentence from a picture.
- [ ] color a picture.
- [ ] Draw a picture.

My sister has nine stuffed animals.

언니는 9 마리의 박제 동물을 가지고 있습니다.

The smiling number nine is saying its name out loud.

웃는 아홉은 그 이름을 크게 말하고있다.

Name

I Can...

- [ ] read the 1st sentence.
- [ ] read the 2nd sentence.
- [ ] make a sentence from a picture.
- [ ] color a picture.
- [ ] Draw a picture.

The baby bee has yellow and black stripes.

아기 꿀벌은 노란색과 검은 색 줄무늬가 있습니다.

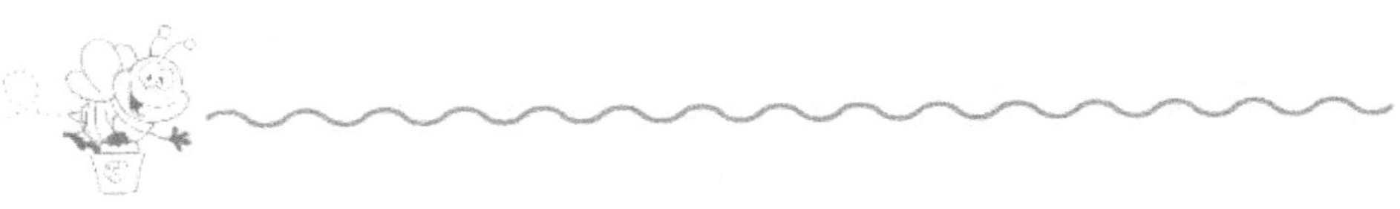

The bee is wearing a pink pacifier to calm itself.

벌은 진정시키기 위해 분홍색 젖꼭지를 입고 있습니다.

Name

I Can...

- [ ] read the 1st sentence.
- [ ] read the 2nd sentence.
- [ ] make a sentence from a picture.
- [ ] color a picture.
- [ ] Draw a picture.

The ladybug has many spots.

무당 벌레에는 많은 반점이 있습니다.

The red and black ladybug is just done eating some leaves.

빨간색과 검은 색 무당 벌레는 잎을
먹기만하면됩니다.

Name

I Can...

- [ ] read the 1st sentence.
- [ ] read the 2nd sentence.
- [ ] make a sentence from a picture.
- [ ] color a picture.
- [ ] Draw a picture.

The sheep are skinny.

양은 마른 체형입니다.

The white sheep have a lot of fluffy white wool to give away.

흰 양에는 푹신한 흰 양모가 많이 나옵니다.

Name

I Can...

- [ ] read the 1st sentence.
- [ ] read the 2nd sentence.
- [ ] make a sentence from a picture.
- [ ] color a picture.
- [ ] Draw a picture.

The rabbit is entering an egg painting contest.

토끼가 달걀 그림 콘테스트에 참가하고 있습니다.

The Easter Bunny is painting a chocolate egg.

부활절 토끼는 초콜릿 달걀을 그림입니다.

Name

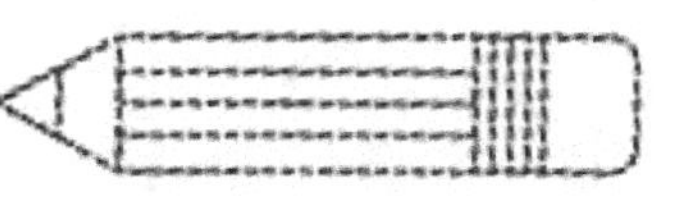

I Can...

- [ ] read the 1st sentence.
- [ ] read the 2nd sentence.
- [ ] make a sentence from a picture.
- [ ] color a picture.
- [ ] Draw a picture.

The owl is a language arts teacher.

올빼미는 언어 예술 교사입니다.

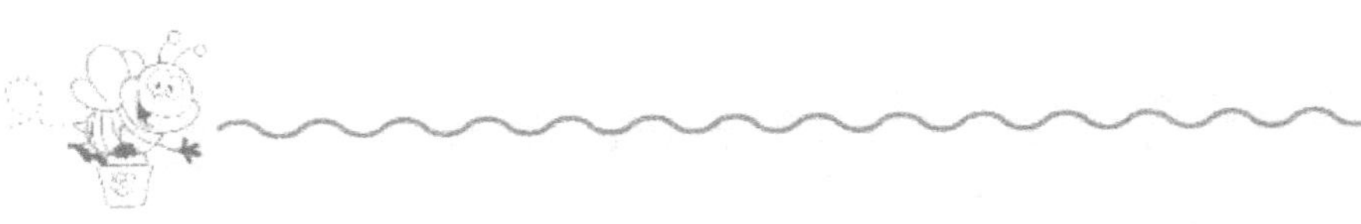

An owl is teaching the kids in school about work.

올빼미는 학교 아이들에게 일에 대해 가르치고 있습니다.

Name ______________

I Can...

- [ ] read the 1st sentence.
- [ ] read the 2nd sentence.
- [ ] make a sentence from a picture.
- [ ] color a picture.
- [ ] Draw a picture.

The man has an ancient hammer.

그 남자는 고대 망치를 가지고있다.

The builder man has gone to work on a project.

건축업자가 프로젝트를 진행했습니다.

Name

I Can...

- [ ] read the 1st sentence.
- [ ] read the 2nd sentence.
- [ ] make a sentence from a picture.
- [ ] color a picture.
- [ ] Draw a picture.

The goat has a friend.

염소는 친구가 있습니다.

The old goat is proud of its golden bell.

오래된 염소는 황금 종을 자랑합니다.

Name

I Can...

- [ ] read the 1st sentence.
- [ ] read the 2nd sentence.
- [ ] make a sentence from a picture.
- [ ] color a picture.
- [ ] Draw a picture.

My mom's friend is a maid.

엄마의 친구는 하녀입니다.

The maid is going to clean the hotel room.

하녀가 호텔 방을 청소하려고합니다.

Name ____________________

I Can...

- ☐ read the 1st sentence.
- ☐ read the 2nd sentence.
- ☐ make a sentence from a picture.
- ☐ color a picture.
- ☐ Draw a picture.

I went to the zoo.

나는 동물원에 갔다.

The animals are having a big celebration.

동물들은 큰 축하를 받고 있습니다.

Name

I Can...

- [ ] read the 1st sentence.
- [ ] read the 2nd sentence.
- [ ] make a sentence from a picture.
- [ ] color a picture.
- [ ] Draw a picture.

The dinosaur has a pillow.

공룡에는 베개가 있습니다.

The dragon is using the rock to build its house.

용은 바위를 사용하여 집을 짓고 있습니다.

Name

I Can...

- [ ] read the 1st sentence.
- [ ] read the 2nd sentence.
- [ ] make a sentence from a picture.
- [ ] color a picture.
- [ ] Draw a picture.

The boy is excited to go to school.

소년은 학교에 갈 것을 기쁘게 생각합니다.

The boy is late for school, so he is sprinting.

소년은 학교에 늦어서 질주하고있다.

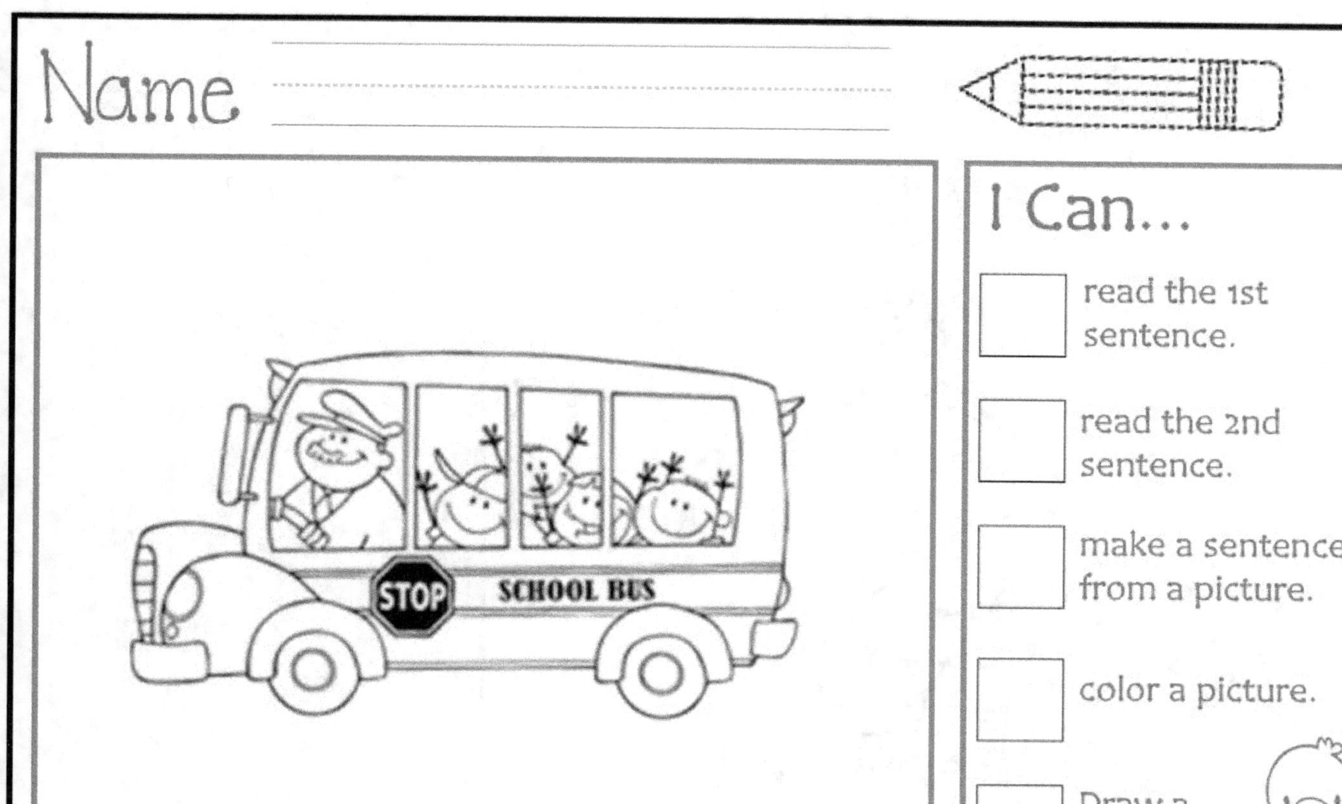

I Can...

- [ ] read the 1st sentence.
- [ ] read the 2nd sentence.
- [ ] make a sentence from a picture.
- [ ] color a picture.
- [ ] Draw a picture.

The kids on the school bus are going to school.

스쿨 버스에있는 아이들이 학교에 다니고 있습니다.

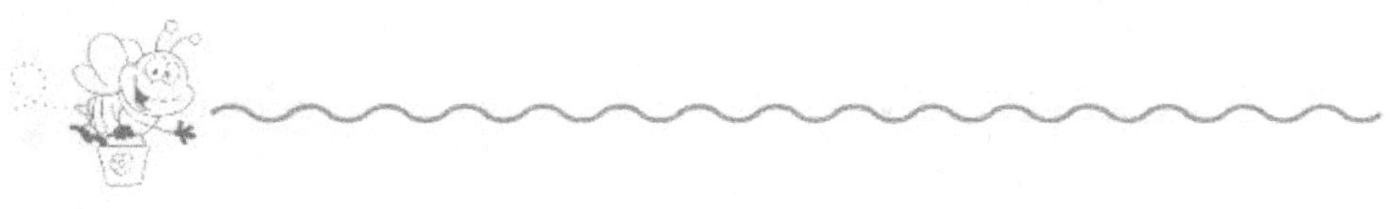

The children are going on a field trip on the yellow bus.

아이들은 노란 버스에서 견학을갑니다.

Name

I Can...

- [ ] read the 1st sentence.
- [ ] read the 2nd sentence.
- [ ] make a sentence from a picture.
- [ ] color a picture.
- [ ] Draw a picture.

The cobra is very lovely.

코브라는 매우 사랑 스럽습니다.

The rattlesnake is looking for its dinner.

방울뱀은 저녁 식사를 찾고 있습니다.

Name

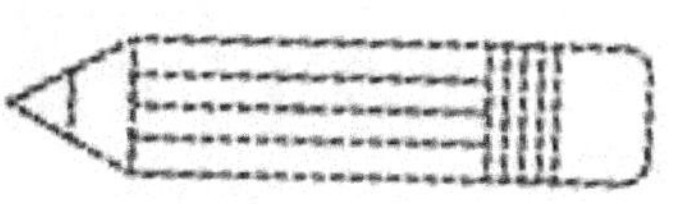

I Can...

- [ ] read the 1st sentence.
- [ ] read the 2nd sentence.
- [ ] make a sentence from a picture.
- [ ] color a picture.
- [ ] Draw a picture.

That is a fat dog!

뚱뚱한 개입니다!

This dog is wagging its tail for more treats.

이 개는 더 많은 간식을 위해 꼬리를 흔들고 있습니다.

Name

I Can...

- [ ] read the 1st sentence.
- [ ] read the 2nd sentence.
- [ ] make a sentence from a picture.
- [ ] color a picture.
- [ ] Draw a picture.

The elephant lives in the zoo.

코끼리는 동물원에 산다.

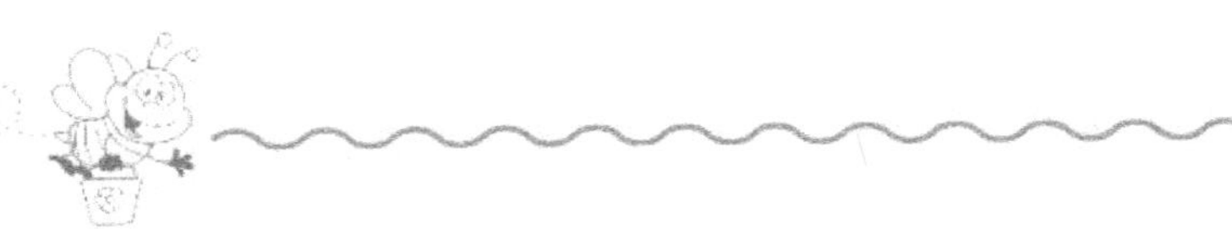

The elephant has a long trunk to spray water.

코끼리는 물을 뿌리기 위해 긴 줄기를 가지고 있습니다.

Name

I Can...

- [ ] read the 1st sentence.
- [ ] read the 2nd sentence.
- [ ] make a sentence from a picture.
- [ ] color a picture.
- [ ] Draw a picture.

The giraffe eats vegetables.

기린은 야채를 먹는다.

The giraffe has an extremely long neck.

기린은 목이 매우 길다.

Name

I Can...

- [ ] read the 1st sentence.
- [ ] read the 2nd sentence.
- [ ] make a sentence from a picture.
- [ ] color a picture.
- [ ] Draw a picture.

The chipmunk has a soft tummy.

다람쥐는 부드러운 배가 있습니다.

The Chipmunk is about to eat a brown acorn.

다람쥐가 갈색 도토리를 먹으려 고합니다.

Name

I Can...

- [ ] read the 1st sentence.
- [ ] read the 2nd sentence.
- [ ] make a sentence from a picture.
- [ ] color a picture.
- [ ] Draw a picture.

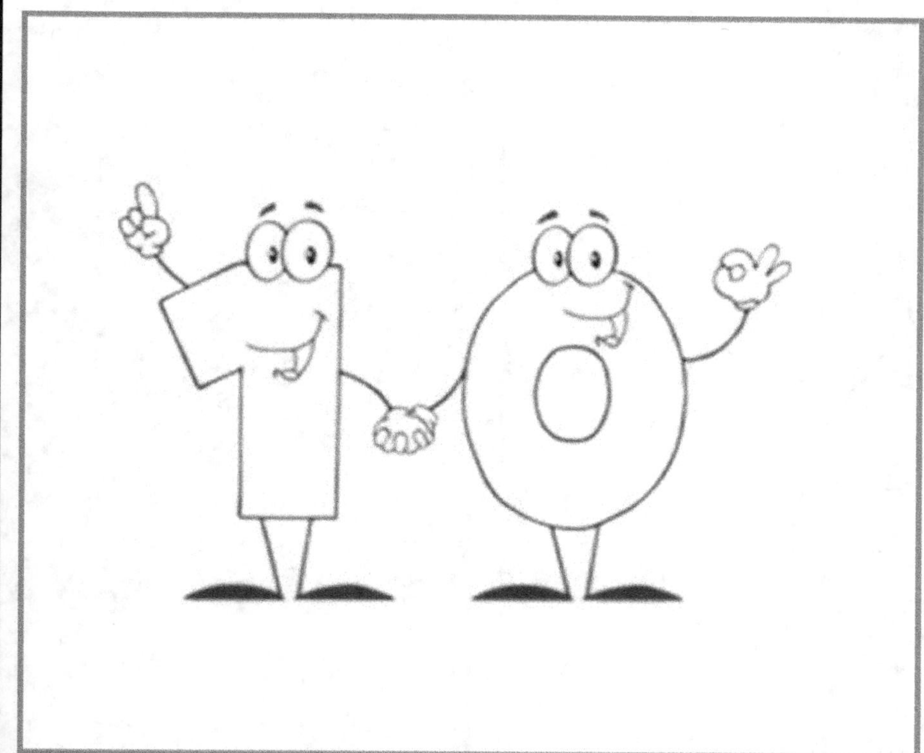

I have ten toes in total.

발가락이 총 10 개 있습니다.

The one and the zero are holding hands.

하나와 제로가 손을 잡고 있습니다.

Name

I Can...

- [ ] read the 1st sentence.
- [ ] read the 2nd sentence.
- [ ] make a sentence from a picture.
- [ ] color a picture.
- [ ] Draw a picture.

The alligator is jumping.

악어가 뛰고있다.

The crocodile is excited.

악어는 흥분된다.

Name

I Can...

- [ ] read the 1st sentence.
- [ ] read the 2nd sentence.
- [ ] make a sentence from a picture.
- [ ] color a picture.
- [ ] Draw a picture.

I found an ant.

나는 개미를 발견했다.

The ant is telling a story.

개미가 이야기를 하고 있습니다.

Name

I Can...

- [ ] read the 1st sentence.
- [ ] read the 2nd sentence.
- [ ] make a sentence from a picture.
- [ ] color a picture.
- [ ] Draw a picture.

The bat sleeps upside down.

박쥐는 거꾸로 잔다.

The bat is ready to fly.

박쥐가 날 준비가되었습니다.

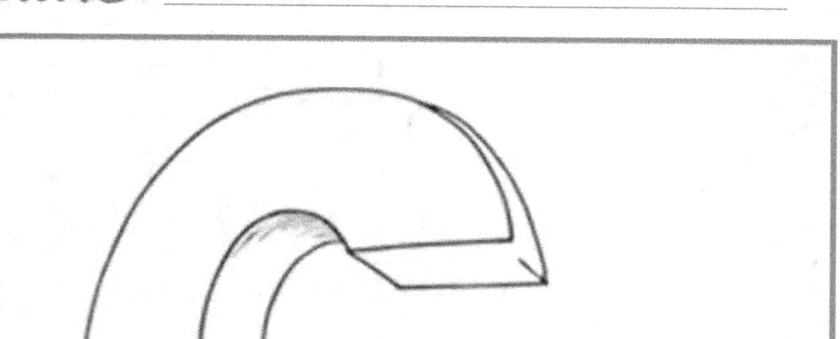

I Can...

- [ ] read the 1st sentence.
- [ ] read the 2nd sentence.
- [ ] make a sentence from a picture.
- [ ] color a picture.
- [ ] Draw a picture.

The cat is very tired.

고양이는 매우 피곤하다.

The cat is taking a nap.

고양이가 낮잠을 자고 있습니다.

Name

I Can...

- [ ] read the 1st sentence.
- [ ] read the 2nd sentence.
- [ ] make a sentence from a picture.
- [ ] color a picture.
- [ ] Draw a picture.

The dog likes to play.

개는 노는 것을 좋아합니다.

The dog is playing with a bone.

개가 뼈를 가지고 놀고있다.

Name

I Can...

- [ ] read the 1st sentence.
- [ ] read the 2nd sentence.
- [ ] make a sentence from a picture.
- [ ] color a picture.
- [ ] Draw a picture.

The elephant has eyelashes.

코끼리는 속눈썹이 있습니다.

The elephant is shy.

코끼리는 부끄러워합니다.

Name

I Can...

- [ ] read the 1st sentence.
- [ ] read the 2nd sentence.
- [ ] make a sentence from a picture.
- [ ] color a picture.
- [ ] Draw a picture.

The frog is hopping.

개구리가 뛰고있다.

The frog is trying to catch the fly.

개구리가 날아 가려고합니다.

Name

I Can...

- [ ] read the 1st sentence.
- [ ] read the 2nd sentence.
- [ ] make a sentence from a picture.
- [ ] color a picture.
- [ ] Draw a picture.

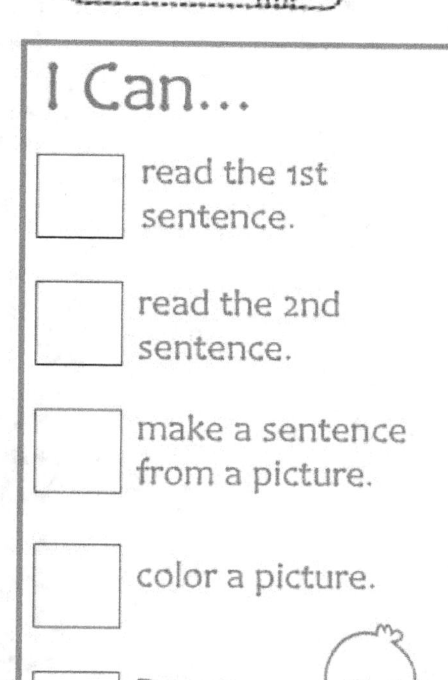

The goat is sleepily walking around.

염소가 잠들고 있습니다.

The goat is eating grass.

염소가 풀을 먹고 있습니다.

Name

I Can...

- [ ] read the 1st sentence.
- [ ] read the 2nd sentence.
- [ ] make a sentence from a picture.
- [ ] color a picture.
- [ ] Draw a picture.

The hippo has a big head.

하마는 큰 머리를 가지고 있습니다.

The hippo has a big head.

하마는 큰 머리를 가지고 있습니다.

I Can...

- [ ] read the 1st sentence.
- [ ] read the 2nd sentence.
- [ ] make a sentence from a picture.
- [ ] color a picture.
- [ ] Draw a picture.

The iguana has a long tail.

이구아나는 꼬리가 길다.

The iguana is hiding behind the letter I.

이구아나는 편지 I 뒤에 숨어 있습니다.

Name

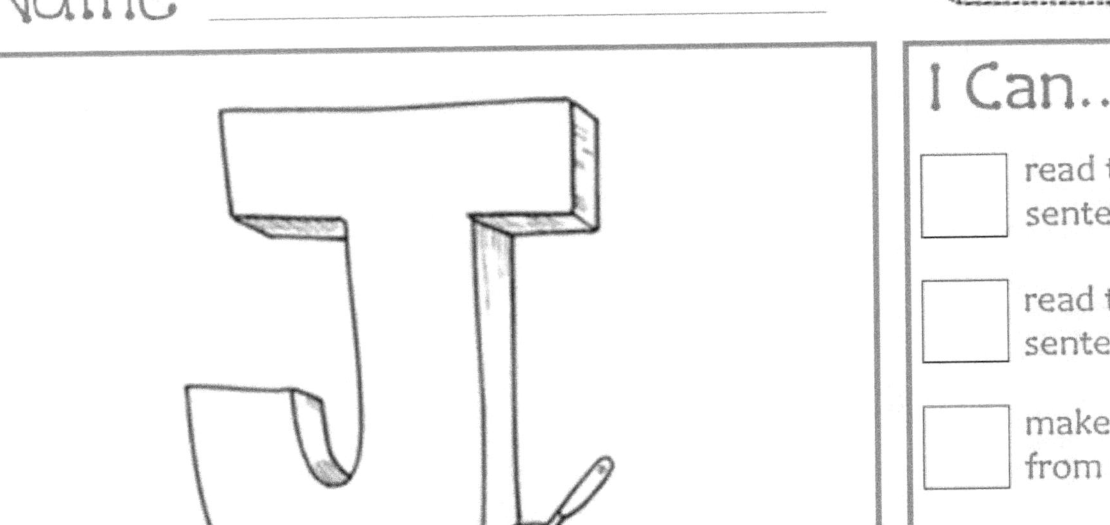

I Can...

- [ ] read the 1st sentence.
- [ ] read the 2nd sentence.
- [ ] make a sentence from a picture.
- [ ] color a picture.
- [ ] Draw a picture.

Mom bought a new bottle of jam.

엄마는 새로운 잼 병을 구입했습니다.

There is jam on the bread.

빵에 잼이 있습니다.

I Can...

- [ ] read the 1st sentence.
- [ ] read the 2nd sentence.
- [ ] make a sentence from a picture.
- [ ] color a picture.
- [ ] Draw a picture.

The kite has a beautiful tail.

연에는 아름다운 꼬리가 있습니다.

The kite is on the ground.

연이 지상에 있습니다.

Name

I Can...

- [ ] read the 1st sentence.
- [ ] read the 2nd sentence.
- [ ] make a sentence from a picture.
- [ ] color a picture.
- [ ] Draw a picture.

The lion is timid.

사자는 소심합니다.

The lion is big.

사자가 크다.

Name 

I Can...

- ☐ read the 1st sentence.
- ☐ read the 2nd sentence.
- ☐ make a sentence from a picture.
- ☐ color a picture.
- ☐ Draw a picture.

I like mice.

나는 쥐를 좋아한다.

A rat is on top of the letter M

쥐가 편지 M 위에있다

Name

I Can...

- [ ] read the 1st sentence.
- [ ] read the 2nd sentence.
- [ ] make a sentence from a picture.
- [ ] color a picture.
- [ ] Draw a picture.

The nose is breathing.

코가 숨 쉬고 있습니다.

The letter N stands for a nose.

문자 N은 코를 나타냅니다.

Name

I Can...

- [ ] read the 1st sentence.
- [ ] read the 2nd sentence.
- [ ] make a sentence from a picture.
- [ ] color a picture.
- [ ] Draw a picture.

The octopus lives underwater.

문어는 수중에 산다.

The octopus has eight tentacles.

문어에는 8 개의 촉수가 있습니다.

Name

I Can...

- [ ] read the 1st sentence.
- [ ] read the 2nd sentence.
- [ ] make a sentence from a picture.
- [ ] color a picture.
- [ ] Draw a picture.

The penguin eats fish.

펭귄은 물고기를 먹는다.

The penguin lives in the arctic.

펭귄은 북극에 산다.

Name

I Can...

- [ ] read the 1st sentence.
- [ ] read the 2nd sentence.
- [ ] make a sentence from a picture.
- [ ] color a picture.
- [ ] Draw a picture.

The queen has a wand.

여왕은 지팡이가 있습니다.

The queen is beautiful.

여왕은 아름답습니다.

Name

I Can...

- [ ] read the 1st sentence.
- [ ] read the 2nd sentence.
- [ ] make a sentence from a picture.
- [ ] color a picture.
- [ ] Draw a picture.

The rabbit has long ears.

토끼는 귀가 길다.

The rabbit is thinking about something.

토끼는 무언가를 생각하고 있습니다.

Name _______________

I Can...

- [ ] read the 1st sentence.
- [ ] read the 2nd sentence.
- [ ] make a sentence from a picture.
- [ ] color a picture.
- [ ] Draw a picture.

The snake has polka dots.

뱀에는 물방울 무늬가 있습니다.

The snake is licking its lip because it is hungry.

뱀은 배가 고파서 입술을 핥고있다.

Name

I Can...

- [ ] read the 1st sentence.
- [ ] read the 2nd sentence.
- [ ] make a sentence from a picture.
- [ ] color a picture.
- [ ] Draw a picture.

The tortoise has a pointy shell.

거북이는 뽀족한 껍질을 가지고 있습니다.

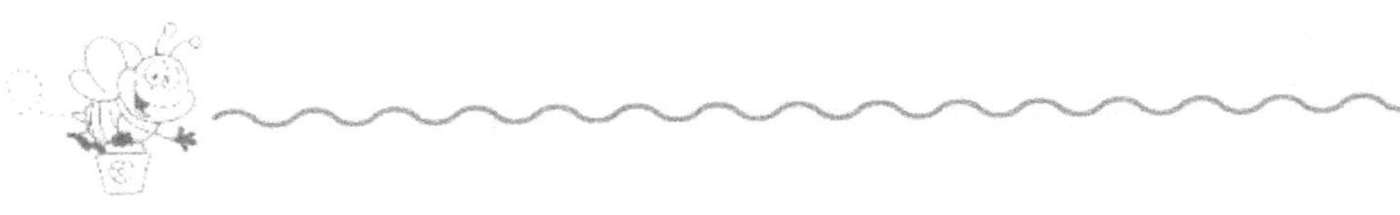

The turtle has a robust shell but is very slow.

거북이는 견고하지만 껍질이 매우 느립니다.

Name

I Can...

- [ ] read the 1st sentence.
- [ ] read the 2nd sentence.
- [ ] make a sentence from a picture.
- [ ] color a picture.
- [ ] Draw a picture.

It's raining.

비가옵니다.

We use the umbrella when it's raining.

비가 올 때 우산을 사용합니다.

Name

I Can...

- [ ] read the 1st sentence.
- [ ] read the 2nd sentence.
- [ ] make a sentence from a picture.
- [ ] color a picture.
- [ ] Draw a picture.

The violin is a musical instrument.

바이올린은 악기입니다.

A violin can play beautiful music if played correctly.

바이올린을 올바르게 연주하면 아름다운 음악을
연주 할 수 있습니다.

I Can...

- [ ] read the 1st sentence.
- [ ] read the 2nd sentence.
- [ ] make a sentence from a picture.
- [ ] color a picture.
- [ ] Draw a picture.

The walrus has a friend.

해마에는 친구가 있습니다.

The walrus has unusually sharp teeth.

해마는 비정상적으로 날카로운 이빨을 가지고 있습니다.

Name

I Can...

- [ ] read the 1st sentence.
- [ ] read the 2nd sentence.
- [ ] make a sentence from a picture.
- [ ] color a picture.
- [ ] Draw a picture.

The xylophone is a colorful instrument.

실로폰은 화려한 악기입니다.

The xylophone is an instrument like the piano.

실로폰은 피아노와 같은 악기입니다.

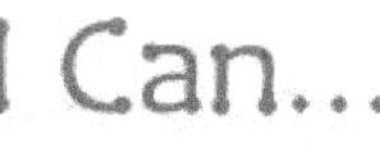

I Can...

- [ ] read the 1st sentence.
- [ ] read the 2nd sentence.
- [ ] make a sentence from a picture.
- [ ] color a picture.
- [ ] Draw a picture.

The boy has a little hat.

소년은 작은 모자를 가지고있다.

The boy is having fun playing with a yoyo.

소년은 요요를 가지고 노는 것을 즐깁니다.

Name

I Can...

- [ ] read the 1st sentence.
- [ ] read the 2nd sentence.
- [ ] make a sentence from a picture.
- [ ] color a picture.
- [ ] Draw a picture.

The zebra has a tail.

얼룩말에는 꼬리가 있습니다.

The zebra has black and white stripes.

얼룩말에는 검은 색과 흰색 줄무늬가 있습니다.

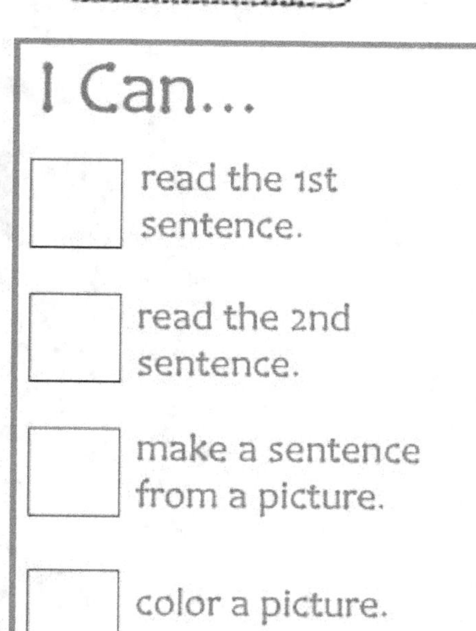

I have a candle on my cake.

케이크에 촛불이 있습니다.

I had a small birthday cake for my party.

나는 파티를 위해 작은 생일 케이크를 먹었다.

I Can...

- [ ] read the 1st sentence.
- [ ] read the 2nd sentence.
- [ ] make a sentence from a picture.
- [ ] color a picture.
- [ ] Draw a picture.

The astronaut is going on a mission.

우주 비행사가 임무를 수행하고 있습니다.

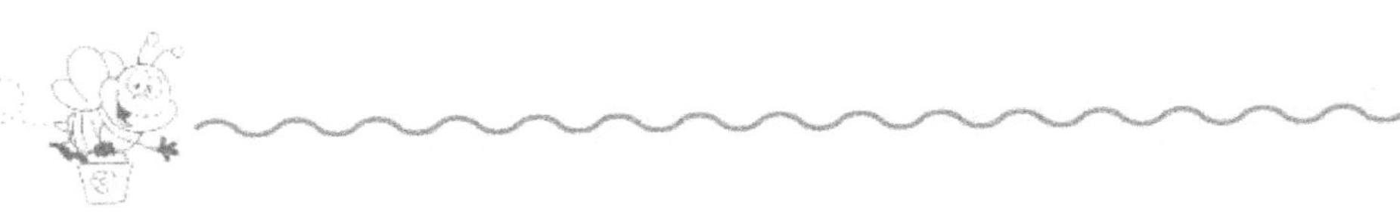

An astronaut has to explore our universe so that we would have more knowledge.

우주 비행사가 더 많은 지식을 갖기 위해 우주를 탐험해야합니다.

Name

I Can...

- [ ] read the 1st sentence.
- [ ] read the 2nd sentence.
- [ ] make a sentence from a picture.
- [ ] color a picture.
- [ ] Draw a picture.

The samurai is going for a morning jog.

사무라이가 아침 조깅을 하려고합니다.

The samurai is training to become good at fighting.

사무라이는 전투에 능숙 해 지도록 훈련하고 있습니다.

Name

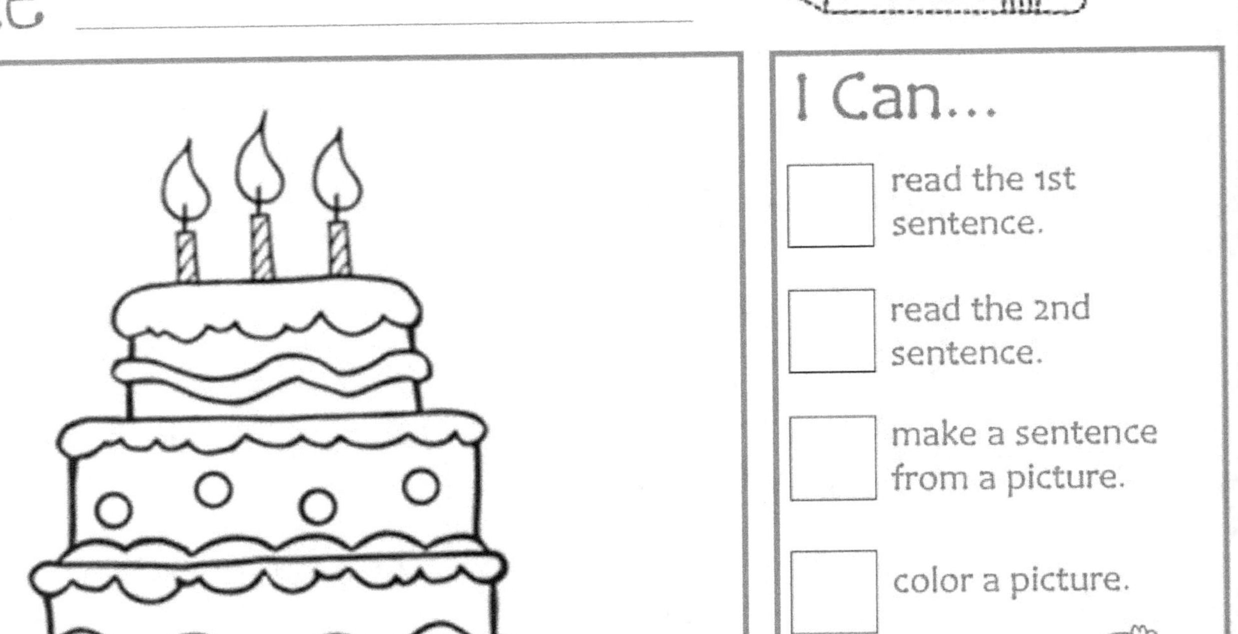

I Can...

- [ ] read the 1st sentence.
- [ ] read the 2nd sentence.
- [ ] make a sentence from a picture.
- [ ] color a picture.
- [ ] Draw a picture.

My friend is having a gigantic cake.

내 친구는 거대한 케이크를 먹고 있습니다.

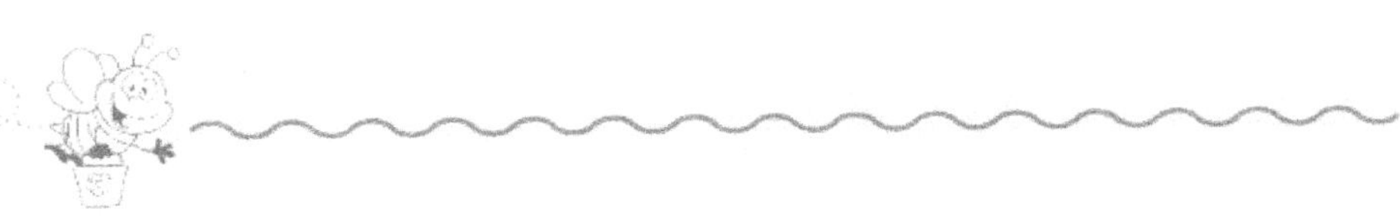

I had a humongous birthday cake for my celebration.

나는 축하를 위해 엄청난 생일 케이크를 먹었다.

Name ________________________ 

I Can...

- [ ] read the 1st sentence.
- [ ] read the 2nd sentence.
- [ ] make a sentence from a picture.
- [ ] color a picture.
- [ ] Draw a picture.

The frog is chasing the fly.

개구리가 날아가고있다

The green frog is trying to catch the fly.

녹색 개구리가 날아 가려고합니다.

Name

I Can...

- [ ] read the 1st sentence.
- [ ] read the 2nd sentence.
- [ ] make a sentence from a picture.
- [ ] color a picture.
- [ ] Draw a picture.

The ladybug has six legs.

무당 벌레에는 6 개의 다리가 있습니다.

The ladybug is on the leaf.

무당 벌레는 잎에 있습니다.

I Can...

- [ ] read the 1st sentence.
- [ ] read the 2nd sentence.
- [ ] make a sentence from a picture.
- [ ] color a picture.
- [ ] Draw a picture.

The dragon is sick.

용은 아프다.

The dragon just ate something spicy, so he needed water.

용은 단지 매운 것을 먹었으므로 물이 필요했습니다.

I Can...

- [ ] read the 1st sentence.
- [ ] read the 2nd sentence.
- [ ] make a sentence from a picture.
- [ ] color a picture.
- [ ] Draw a picture.

That is a baby cow.

그것은 아기 젖소입니다.

A little cow is walking around near the barn.

작은 암소가 헛간 근처를 걷고있다.

Name

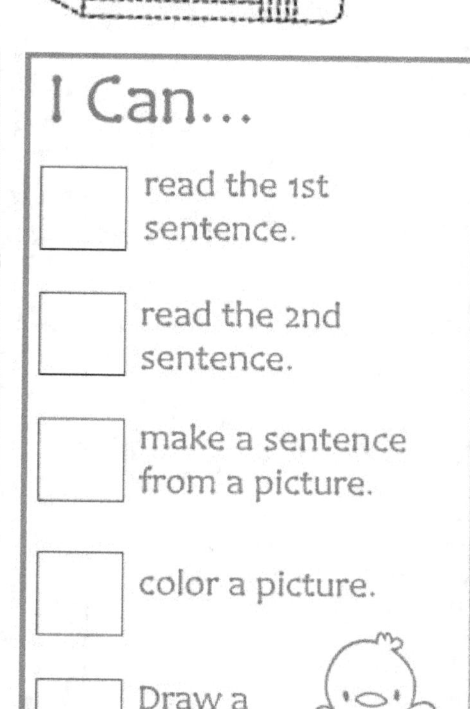

I Can...

- [ ] read the 1st sentence.
- [ ] read the 2nd sentence.
- [ ] make a sentence from a picture.
- [ ] color a picture.
- [ ] Draw a picture.

The frog has a big smile.

개구리는 큰 웃음을 가지고있다.

The frog is smiling because it is happy.

개구리는 행복하기 때문에 웃고 있습니다.

Name

I Can...

- [ ] read the 1st sentence.
- [ ] read the 2nd sentence.
- [ ] make a sentence from a picture.
- [ ] color a picture.
- [ ] Draw a picture.

The frog has a big mouth.

개구리는 큰 입을 가지고 있습니다.

The frog is waving to us.

개구리가 우리에게 손을 흔든다.

www.ingramcontent.com/pod-product-compliance
Lightning Source LLC
Chambersburg PA
CBHW080836160726

47999CB00009B/2906